„I am"

62 Positive Affirmations for Happiness and Self-Love

Alexi Divine

Disclaimer Notice:
The information in this book is intended for educational and entertainment purposes only.

ISBN: 9798860255319
Imprint: Independently published

Introduction to this affirmation book

The affirmations provided in this book are very simple but powerful.

The world can be overwhelming, situations we meet everyday stressful.
Sometimes you may not accept yourself or even be angry at yourself. With so many things out of control, we must focus on what we can control – our own thoughts and minds.

When you have more positive thoughts about yourself, then you can attract more good things to your life.
Affirmations are positive statements to make you feel loved and happy. By practicing those affirmations daily, you have the power to create a new you.
You can have better results if you practice reading it together with writing and creating a new version of yourself.

Please do not forget to visualize that you are already this person and you have everything you ever desire.

Sure, repeating those phrases to yourself may seem a little weird. But trust me. Together with my notebook I have created for you to write your gratitude and affirmations daily , it pays off in the run.

Remember to practise daily for minimum of 40 days.

„I am" affirmations are essential for developing a sense of self – awareness and self – love.
Wouldn't you love to accept everything about yourself? Feel confident about yourself?

In the words of Ru Paul, „If you can't love yourself, how the hell are you going to love someone else?
If you are skeptical of the process, there is no harm in giving it a try.
You are only asked to read affirmations twice a day and also visualise each affirmation as if is already present. When you add writing them down, I am sure you will feel happier within few days.
Are you ready for your new life?

To all wonderful women on this planet.

If you can dream it, then you can achieve it.

'Zig Ziglar'

I am a wonderful person

I am
beautiful

I am amazing

I am good
with myself

I am
powerful

I am
loved

I am
happy

I am successful in everything I do

I am grateful for everything I have

I am unique
in this world

I am worthy of love and appreciation

I am
wealthy

I am capable

I am
healthy

I am creating
my own life

I am
blessed

I am
strong

I let go all criticism and negativity

I am in love with who I am right now

I am confident

I am patient

I am aware of my strengths

I am motivated by my goals

I am kind
and caring

I am good enough

I am
safe

I am smart
and
intelligent

I am
guided in my
life

I am protected

I am talented and creative

I am
important

I am
relaxed

I am free

I am
abundant

I am
magnificent

I am joyful for every moment

I am
unstoppable

I am positive

I believe in myself

I am courageous

I am always
in the right
place at the
right time

I am
financially
independent

I am surrounded by love

I am proud of my life choices

I am giving myself the love I deserve

I am
calm

I am learning from every situation in my life

I am fully responsible for my happiness

I am prosperous

I am attracting money and wealth

I am proud of
myself

I can forgive myself and others

I am
wise

I am in control of my thoughts and emotions

I am aware I
can achieve
everything

I am
cheerful

I am ok with
my
imperfections

I am doing
my best

I am open to receive

I am worthy
of success

I am a
money
magnet

I am bountiful

I love
myself

Notes. Your own affirmations

Notes. Your own affirmations

Notes. Your own affirmations

Thank you for purchasing this book. I hope you enjoyed it.

More similar projects you can find on:

USA

UK

Printed in Great Britain
by Amazon